KU-538-503

TATTOO

TATTOO

HUNDREDS OF TATTOO DESIGN IDEAS

Silverdale Books

This Silverdale Books edition is published by
66 Books Ltd
66 Wood Lane End
Hemel Hempstead
Hertfordshire HP2 4RF
United Kingdom

Produced on behalf of 66 Books by
Anness Publishing Ltd
Blaby Road
Wigston
Leicestershire LE18 4SE
Email: info@anness.com
Web: www.annesspublishing.com

ETHICAL TRADING POLICY
Because of Anness Publishing's ongoing ecological investment programme, you, as our customer, can have the pleasure and reassurance of knowing that a tree is being cultivated on your behalf to naturally replace the materials used to make the book you are holding. For further information about this scheme, go to www.annesspublishing.com/trees

© 66 Books Ltd 2012

All rights reserved. No part of this publication may be reproduced, stored in a retrieval system, or transmitted in any way or by any means, electronic, mechanical, photocopying, recording or otherwise, without the prior written permission of the copyright holder.

A CIP catalogue record for this book is available from the British Library.

PUBLISHER'S NOTE
Although the advice and information in this book are believed to be accurate and true at the time of going to press, neither the authors nor the publisher can accept any legal responsibility or liability for any errors or omissions that may have been made nor for any inaccuracies nor for any loss, harm or injury that comes about from following instructions or advice in this book.

CONTENTS

THE ORIGINS OF TATTOOS

The word 'tattoo' is derived from the Polynesian word (either Samoan or Tahitian, depending on the source) – tatau – used to describe the permanent skin markings used by indigenous peoples of the South Pacific islands. But tattooing has been used for centuries in cultures as diverse as the Berber tribes of North Africa, the Ainu people of Japan and the Maoris of New Zealand. Evidence of tattoos has been found on Egyptian mummies from 2000 BC and it is thought that the early peoples of northern Europe also had tattoos often using woad, a traditional blue dye.

In the modern era, the practice of tattooing was popularized in the Western world by sailors, who copied the Polynesian people they had encountered in their journeys of exploration in the 18th century.

THE MEANING OF TATTOOS

Throughout history and across cultures, tattoos have been used to mark status, display religious devotion, celebrate bravery and virility, bring good fortune or proclaim love. And in essence they are used in much the same way in the modern world, although many contemporary tattoo wearers would add beautification of the body to this list.

CHOOSING TO HAVE A TATTOO

The most important thing to remember when deciding to get tattooed is that this is permanent. It's not like having a new hairstyle or colour that will eventually grow out. You have to go into it knowing that you and those close to you will have to live with your tattoo for ever. Yes, tattoos can sometimes be removed, but this is not always successful and can leave a certain amount of scarring. Never get a tattoo with the thought in your mind that you could have it removed later.

THE PLACEMENT OF TATTOOS

You can in theory create a tattoo on any area of skin. The area in which you choose to have your tattoo will be dictated by a number of factors, mainly the size of the design you have selected and whether you want the tattoo to be visible in all types of clothing. Some designs are most suitable for specific parts of the body perhaps because of the natural shape or contours of the area.

FINDING A DESIGN

It's worth spending time thinking carefully about the design. Even the simplest of tattoos involve a design decision whether in terms of the colour, style of lettering or dimensions and shape. Think about the 'look' you want to create classic, gothic, cartoon, etc., and then do your research. You may need to find out what icons or symbols best represent the message you want to convey for example, 'love' or 'peace'. Or perhaps you are attracted by the idea of having a tattoo based on a Chinese character. In this case be sure to find out the exact meaning of the character you are considering in order to avoid a potentially embarrassing mistake.

USING THIS BOOK

You've got this book and that's a great start. You'll find plenty of ideas here to fuel your imagination. You can use the outlines as shown to provide a guide for your tattooist or you can create composite designs by assembling several different elements.

Some of the designs in this book that are shown in black and white, can, of course, be rendered in the combination of colours of your choice. And the scale of the images can be adapted to suit the size of the tattoo you want, which may in turn be determined by the part of the body for which it is intended. But remember that very detailed designs may not be suitable for use on a small scale.

TATTOO IDEAS

ANCHORS

Traditionally, the anchor was a symbol of a crossing, by boat or ship, of the Atlantic Ocean. Anchor tattoos are one of the oldest type of tattoo and were commonly viewed as a symbol of a very experienced sailor. Nowadays, no such restrictions are in place, and people now view the anchor as a symbol of stability and a strong foundation. Today many people get anchor tattoos with their partner's name on it to show their commitment.

HEAVY ANCHOR

ANCHOR AND CHAIN

ANCHOR AND ROPE

BLACK ANCHOR

CHAINED ANCHOR

COMMERCIAL ANCHOR

SPLIT ANCHOR

ANCHOR AND FISH

ANCHOR AND SEA SERPENT

ANCHOR GLOW

ANCHOR AND WHEEL

ANCHOR AND SMALL WHEEL

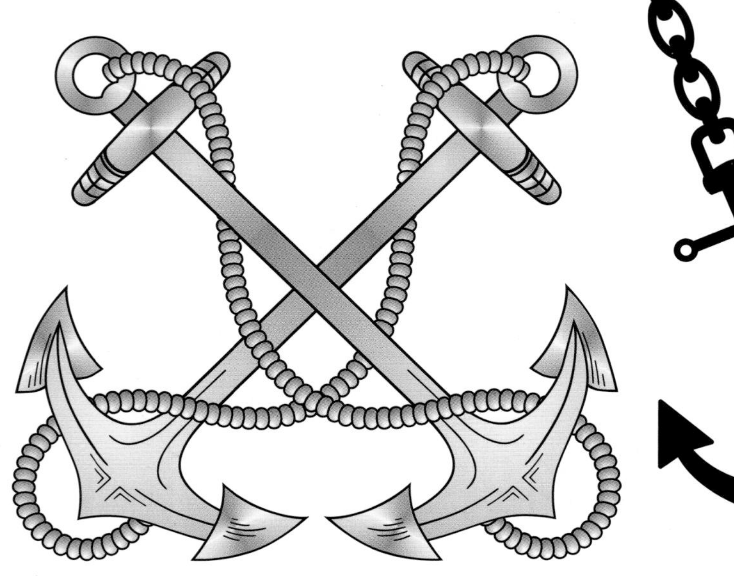

CROSSED ANCHORS

TRADITIONAL ANCHOR

TRIBAL ANCHOR

ABSTACT ANCHOR

ANCHOR CHAIN

ANGELS

Angels are popular tattoos particularly with females, often seen as cherubs in clouds. Angels convey a very spiritual message and are perceived to be the guardians of souls. Throughout history, angels have been depicted as winged creatures, with flowing robes, suffused in light and you can find many wonderful images of Angels to help you in your quest to find the right one for your tattooist. Often you will find an Angel is used either on its own or as a centrepiece of a tattoo intended as a memorial.

CUPID

DIVINE INSPIRATION

DANCING CHERUB I

DANCING CHERUB II

SEATED CHERUB

CHERUB AND HEART

CHERUB AND SCROLL

CHERUB WITH BRANCHES

CHERUB DECORATION

AUTOMOTIVE

Cars are often seen as a symbol of excitement, freedom and raw power. Often in tattoos, images of engines, badges or cars themselves are tempered with a blaze of fire to help instil that undeniable feeling of power and excitement created by fast cars.

WHEEL IN FLAMES

ENGINE POWER

WINGED POWER

SKULL AND CROSSBONES FLAG

WINGED SKULL
WITH ENGINE

CHEQUERED FLAGS

FLAMING CAR I

FLAMING CAR II

FLAMING CAR III

FLAMING CAR IV

FLAMING SYMMETRY I

SKULL ON WHEELS

FLAMING SYMMETRY II

SKULL TORQUE

AZTEC

With their distinctive style made up of bold, geometric shapes, Aztec tattoo designs feature some of the most striking patterns used in tattoo art. The Aztec culture had many powerful gods and the people showed their religious devotion by having tattoos. These indicated their rank and status, and also celebrated a warrior's accomplishments. The placement of the Aztec tattoos indicated which god was celebrated. Wrist, chest and stomach were the most popular body parts for tattoos. These areas are said to be the seats of power.

AZTEC HEAD

MAD MONKEY

STANDING BIRD

OUTSTRETCHED WINGS

STYLIZED EAGLE

AZTEC COMPOSITE

AZTEC BORDER

TORTOISE

WALKING BIRD

LIZARD

BIRD COMPOSITE

RAMPANT DRAGON

DRAGON SNAKE

STORK
FEATHERED
HEADDRESS
MONKEY

BANNERS

Banners and pennants are a popular motif. They provide a decorative way of displaying words, whether the name of a special person in your life or that of your favourite football team. Based on a ribbon design, variations in banner design can include the number and shape of the swirls and kinks, as well as the width and length, and any additional surrounding decoration that may be added.

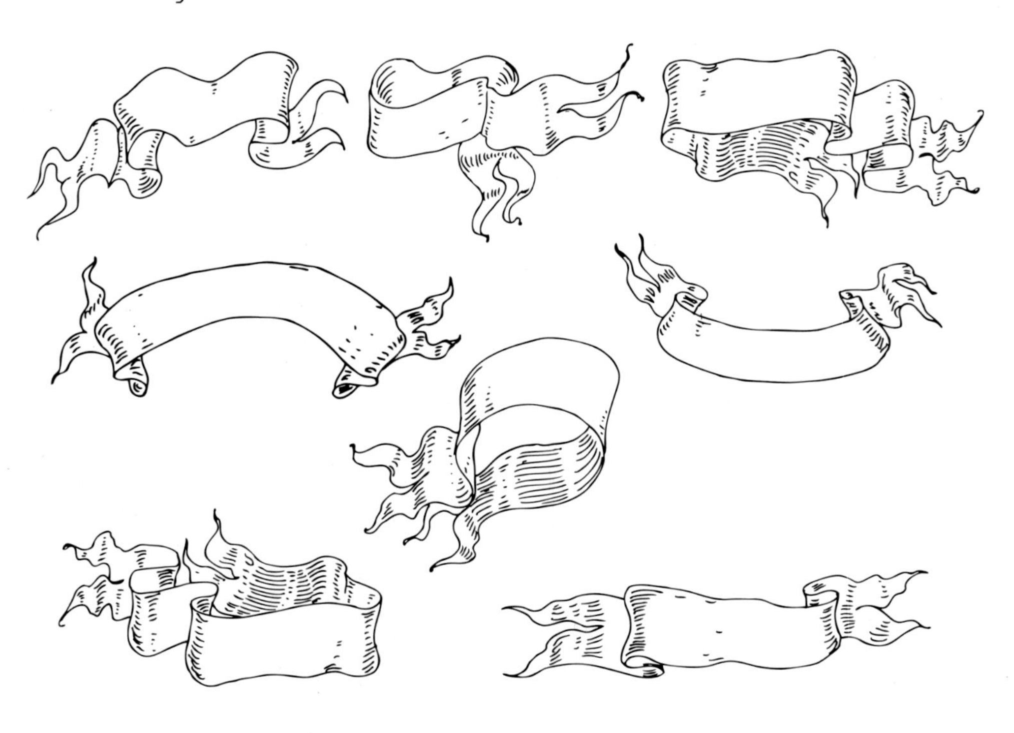

ETCHED BANNERS 1

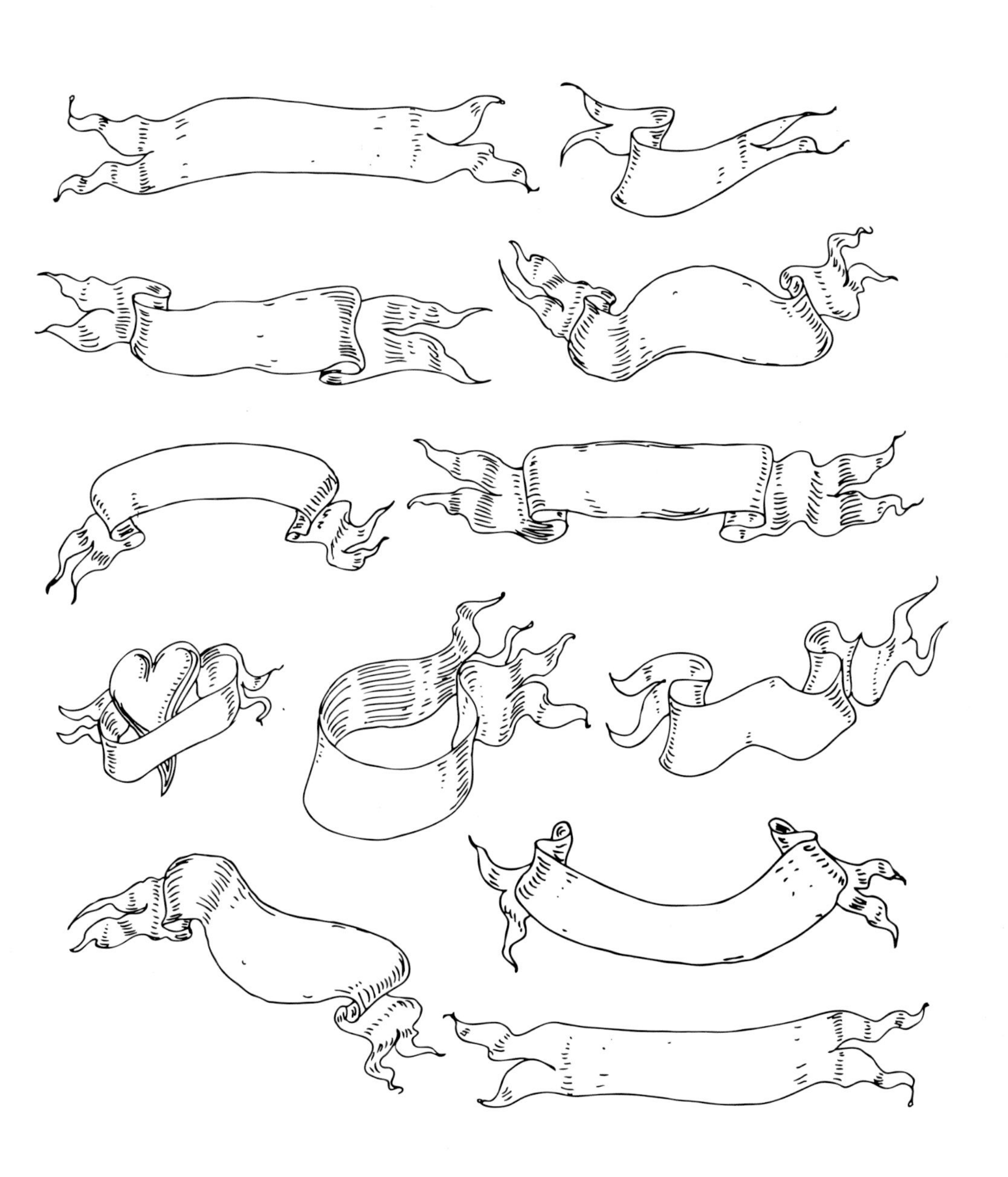

ETCHED BANNERS II

FLOURISHED BANNER

WINGED HEART BANNER

LAUREL BANNER

BATS

Chinese bat tattoos are said to be a symbol of good fortune, and can be used individually or as a group. Five bats on a tattoo symbolize the five types of happiness – peace, riches, love of virtue, long life and happy death. Bat tattoos are also often associated with vampires, so you could find tattoos where the bat is sinking sharp fangs into the skin of the owner, or even transforming itself into a fierce vampire.

CHINESE BAT

5 LUCKY BATS

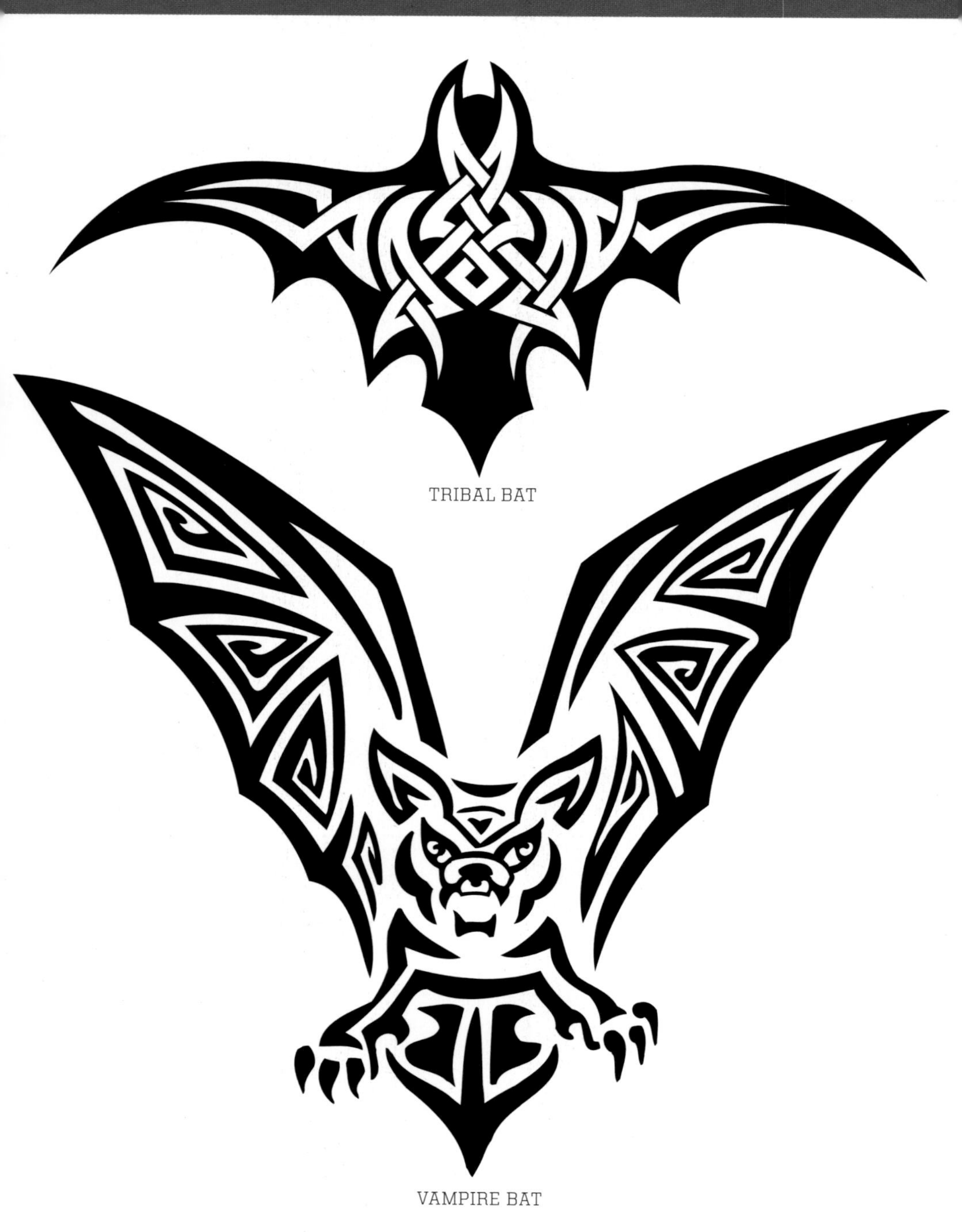

TRIBAL BAT

VAMPIRE BAT

OUTSTRETCHED BAT

SPOOOKY BAT

NIGHT FLIGHT

HOT VAMPIRE

HAPPY VAMPIRE

GRINNING VAMPIRE

DEMON BAT

BIRDS

A bird in flight symbolizes lightness of spirit and hope. They can inspire very beautiful, powerful tattoos. There are many species of birds to choose from and as each bird has its own specific symbolism, it is important to do some research on your chosen bird before going to the tattoo parlour.

Some examples of bird meanings are the dove for peace and tranquillity, the robin for spring, youth or even new life, and the bluebird for happiness. Swallow tattoos were common among sailors, who regarded this bird as a representation of their wanderlust. According to some sources, sailors would often have a swallow tattoo after spending 5,000 miles at sea.

In modern culture, eagles are a symbol of liberty, freedom and strength. Owls are a popular tattoo choice, representing wisdom, psychic energy and spirituality.

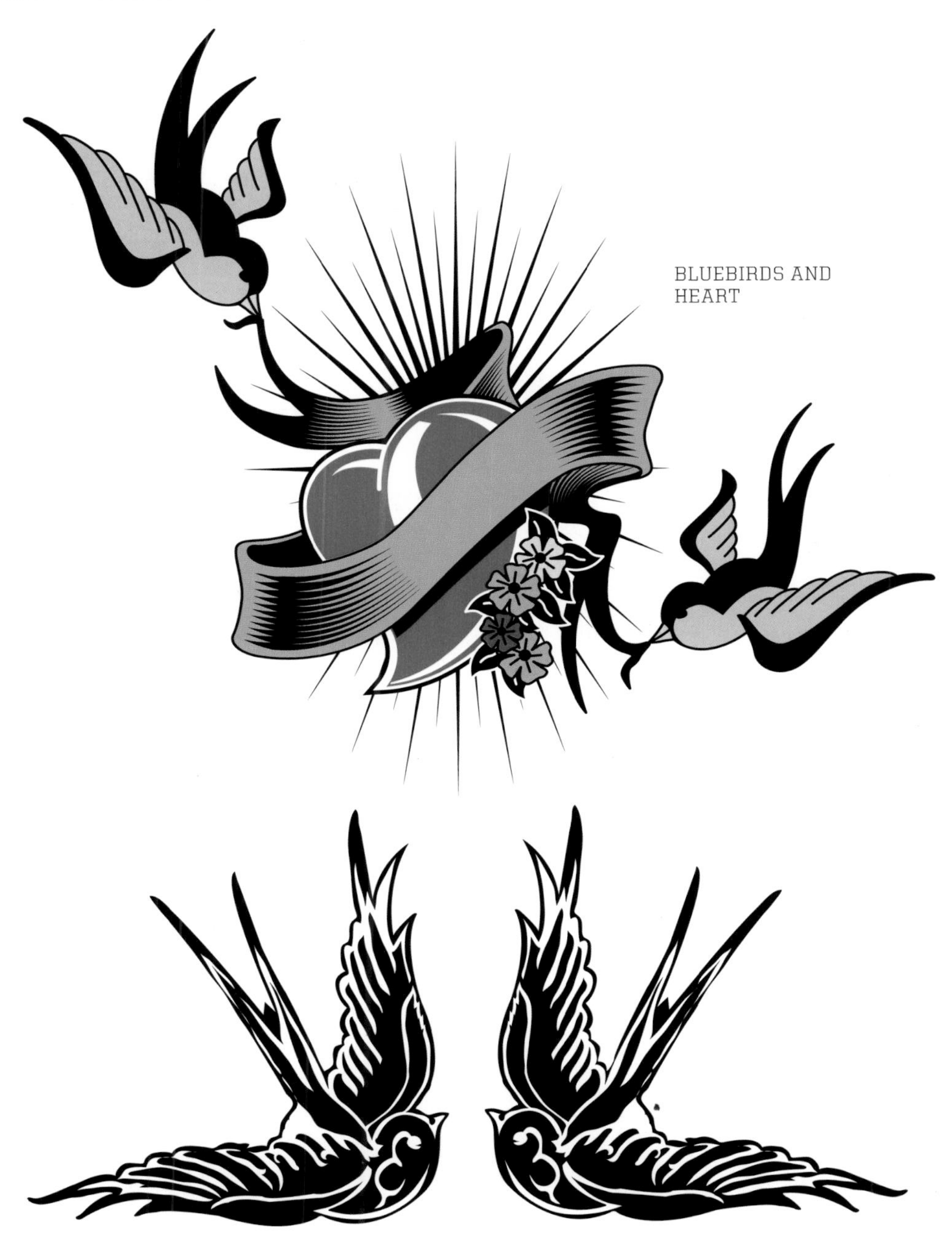

BLUEBIRDS AND HEART

SWALLOWS

FLYING HIGH

FEATHERED FLIGHT

SOARING SPIRIT

SKYLARK

RAINBOW BIRD

COCKEREL

CHICKEN FLIGHT

KINGFISHER

FIRE EAGLE

STOMPING AROUND

ROOSTER

MINIMALIST OWL

OWL SWOOP

BLACK OWL

WHITE OWL

OWL WITH WINGS SPREAD

OWL WITH WINGS RAISED

OWL STARE

TU-WHIT TU-WHOO

VULTURE

RAINING FIRE

HAWK'S HEAD

AIRLINE

HAWKEYE

COLD STARE

HARPY EAGLE

EAGLE EYES

EAGLE SWOOSH

FIRE DOWN

FEATHERED LANDING

SHARP EYES

BALD EAGLE

SNAKE CATCHER

BUTTERFLIES

The butterfly is a symbol of transformation. Tattoos of these beautiful and graceful creatures are incredibly popular among women for their delicacy. There are literally thousands of varieties of butterflies, so you will have endless options to choose from, either an actual butterfly or an abstract design. Most designs are done on the lower back, shoulder or ankle.

MOTH

TRIBAL BUTTERFLY

NATURE'S BEAUTIES

OWL-EYED BUTTERFLY

HEART TAIL

MONARCH BUTTERFLY

SWALLOWTAIL

PEACOCK BUTTERFLY

RAGGED-TAILED BUTTERFLY

SURF BUTTERFLY
DREAMTAIL

OWL BUTTERFLY

PINK METALLIC

PAISLEYFLY

BLACK ADMIRAL

WHITE ADMIRAL

TWISTED BUTTERFLY

BRITISH BLUE

IRON-WING BUTTERFLIES

CATS

Independent, proud and sleek are some of the many adjectives used to describe cats and there are multitudes of cat tattoo designs to choose from, ranging from the domestic cat to the big cats of the wild. Effective cat tattoos can be created from a stylized image, a silhouette or a realistic rendering of one of these majestic creatures. Lions, cheetahs, tigers and pumas are popular tattoos representing strength and courage. Many men opt for tattoos of the big cats to express their strength and masculinity. Cats are also popular tattoos for women, representing a woman's nurturing instincts and her fearless defence of her family.

LYNX HEAD

BLACK CAT

WITCH'S CAT

LION AND BANNER

CHINESE TIGER

CAT SNARL

YELLOW EYES

TIGER'S ROAR

TIGER PRIDE

COOL STARE

TIGER RAMPANT

BANNER-WRAPPED TIGER

STALKING TIGER

WILD CAT

BOBCAT

BOBCAT ROAR

BOBCAT FACE

LION IN THE WIND

LION IN THE ROUND

LION HEAD

LION HEAD SIDE

CELTIC

The Celtic knot has a universal appeal. It is commonly used in armband style tattoos. This does not need to be a limited design though; Celtic knotwork forms can easily be transformed into anything in the hands of a good artist. There are similar designs from many other parts of the world. In Tibet and Nepal these designs represent the continuity of life.

CELTIC CHAINS

CELTIC ICONS

CELTIC MOON

CELTIC PATTERN I

CELTIC PATTERN II

CELTIC CIRCLE

CELTIC KNOTS

CELTIC KNOTS

CELTIC CROSS

CELTIC ANIMALS

CELTIC CIRCLE CROSS

CHINESE

As some of the most exotic and mysterious tattoos, Chinese writing tattoos are more popular than ever before. The wide appeal lies in the fact that their meanings are hidden from observers (unless they can read Chinese) and the artful strokes that make up each character are appealing to the eye. Most commonly tattooed using black ink, Chinese writing tattoos make bold statements and are often chosen in the West to express ideals and admired qualities, to spell out words that are meaningful to the owner, or the names of loved ones.

I LOVE YOU

GOOD FORTUNE

PROSPERITY

LONGEVITY

AUSPICIOUSNESS

狗
DOG
猪
PIG
鼠
RAT
羊
GOAT
龙
DRAGON
猴
MONKEY
蛇
SNAKE
虎
TIGER
牛
OX
鸡
ROOSTER
兔
RABBIT
马
HORSE

CIRCLES

One of the most basic shapes, a circle is often used in a tattoo as a simple border design to enclose another motif. However, the decoration of the circumference can provide visual interest in its own right, often incorporating motifs that link it to the content or meaning of the item it surrounds.

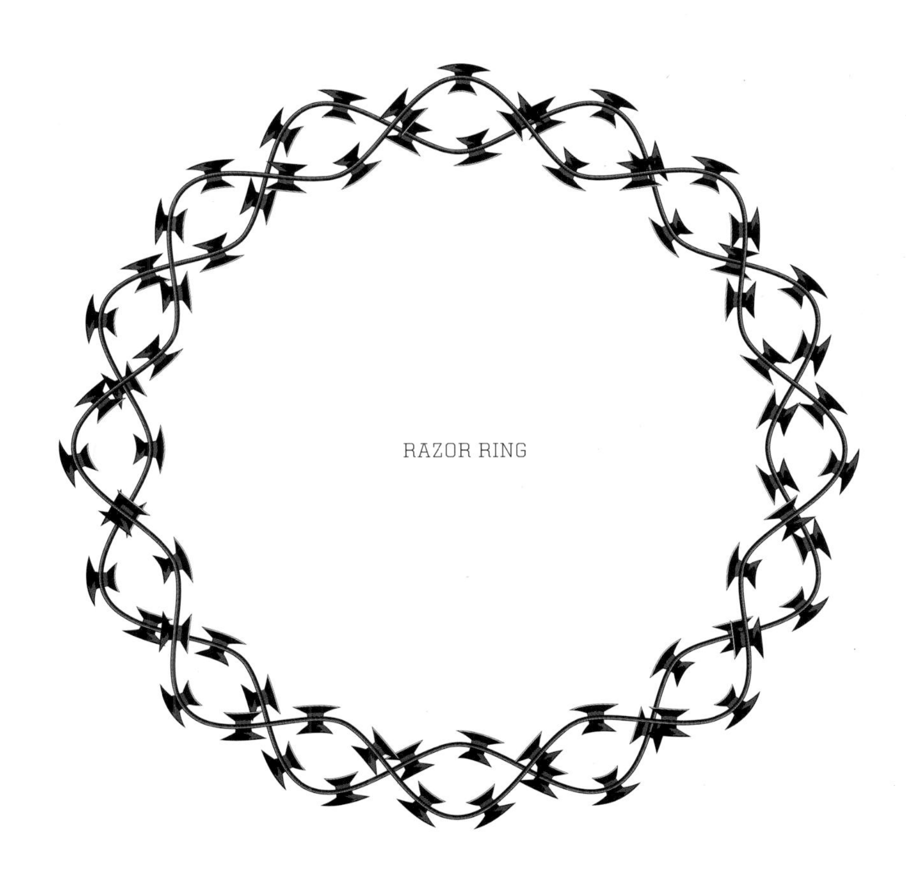

RAZOR RING

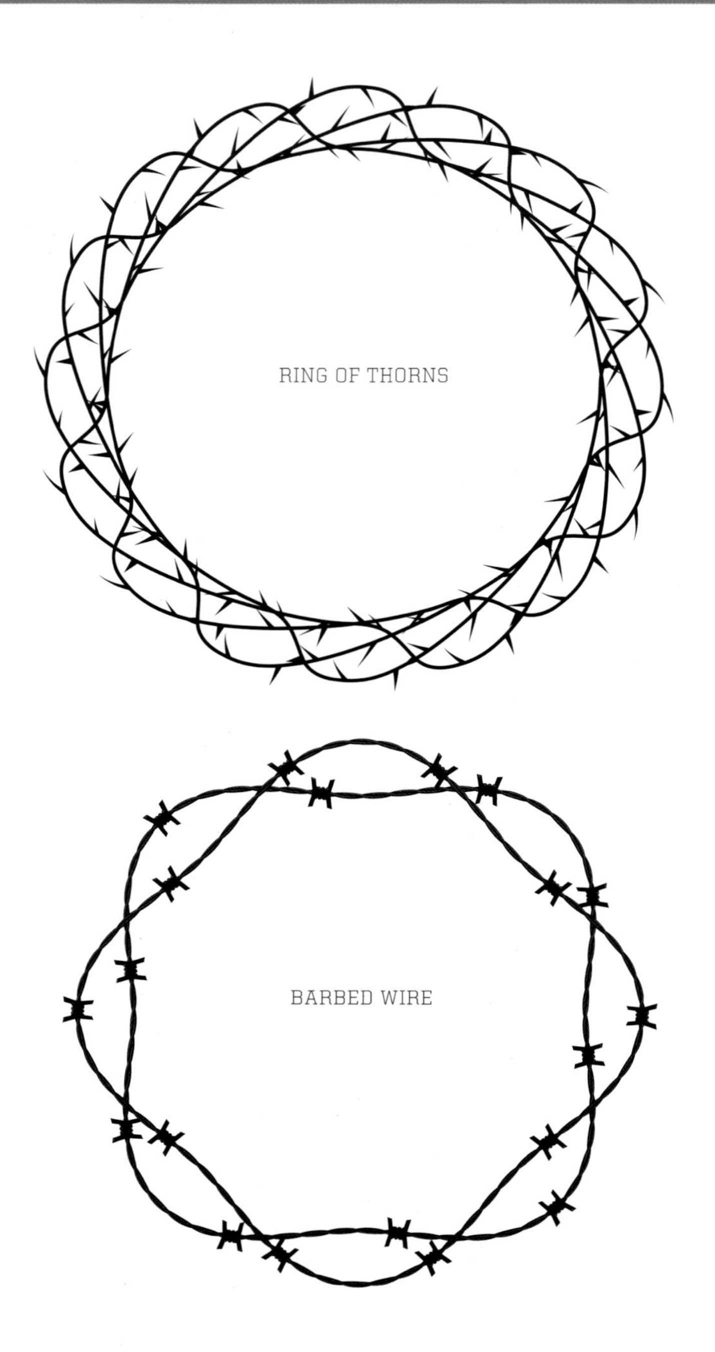
RING OF THORNS
BARBED WIRE

CELTIC CIRCLE

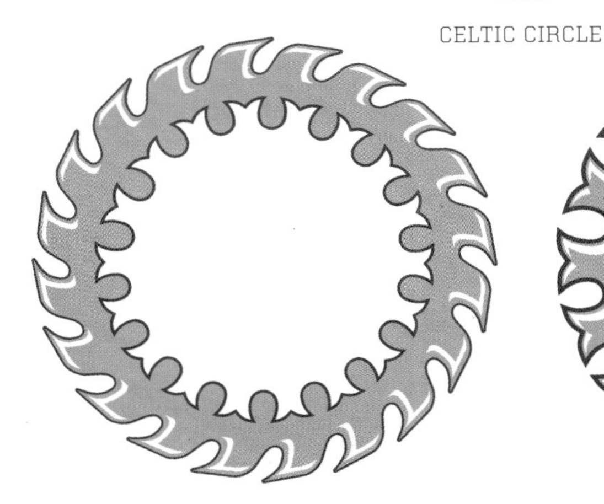

SAW BLADE

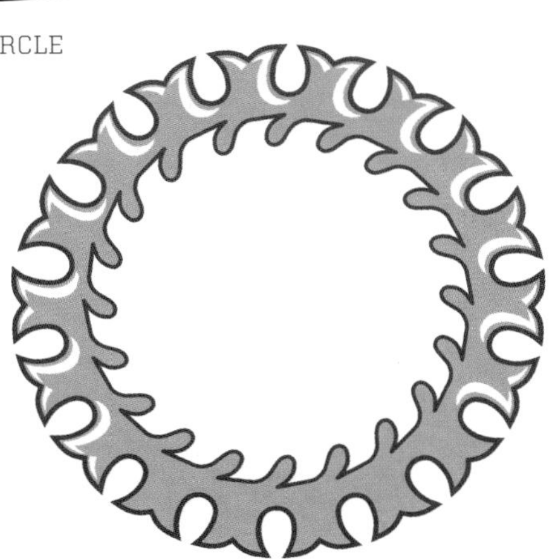

CUTTING RING

CROCODILES

Frightening in the wild, a crocodile in a tattoo design also carries with it a sense of danger. Its strong and sinuous body and wide jaw packed with large, pointed teeth, provide plenty of design possibilities for the tattoo artist.

TRIBAL CROC

GAPING CROC

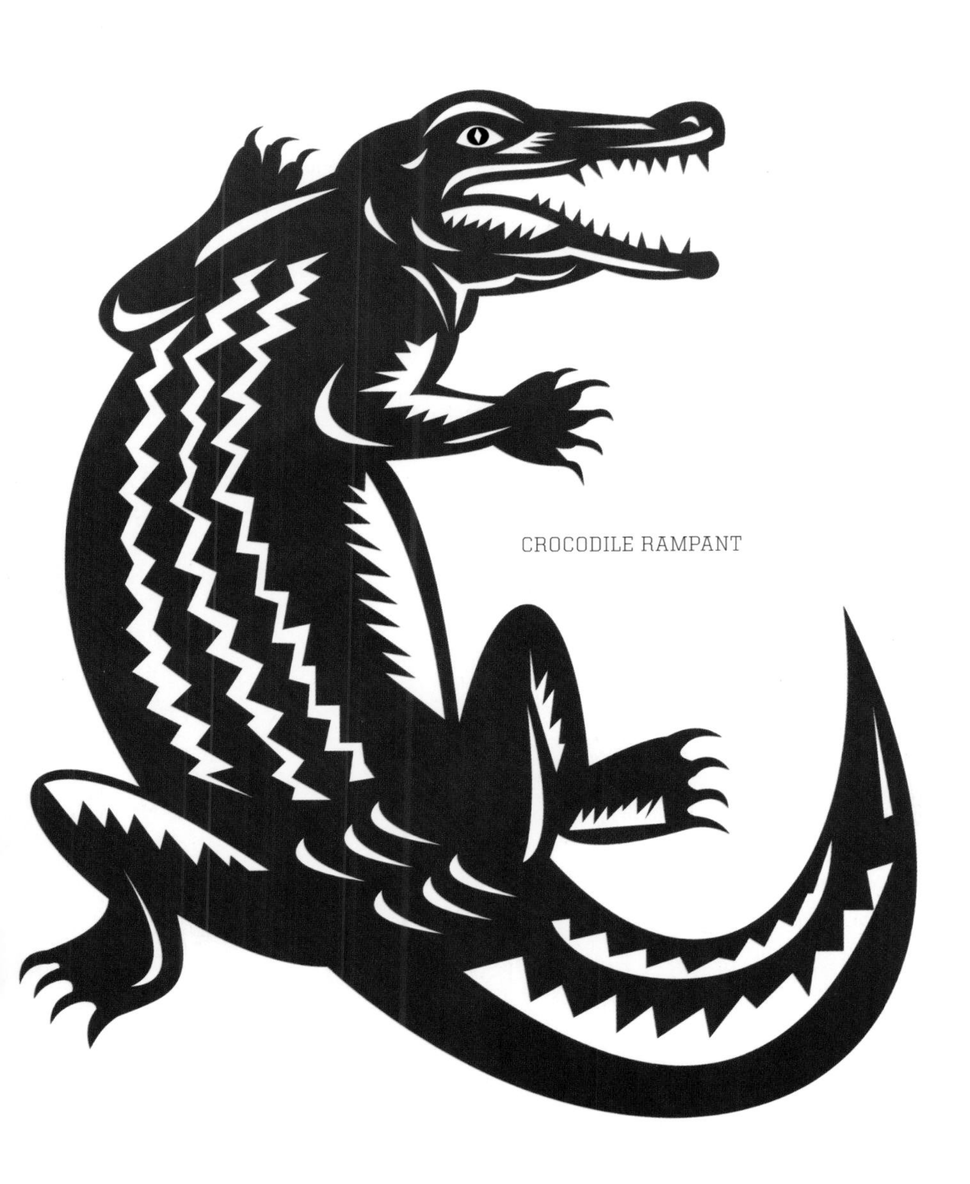

CROCODILE RAMPANT

DOGS

Having a dog tattoo is often seen as a display of love and affection for a canine companion, who has passed away. In Shamanism, they associate the dog with the powers of the forest, strong and steadfast guiding us through mystical territory, the dog being a guide through the journey. Dog tattoos therefore can also convey a companion is guiding you through a journey, either spiritual or physical. In Asian culture, the dog is perceived to be good luck.

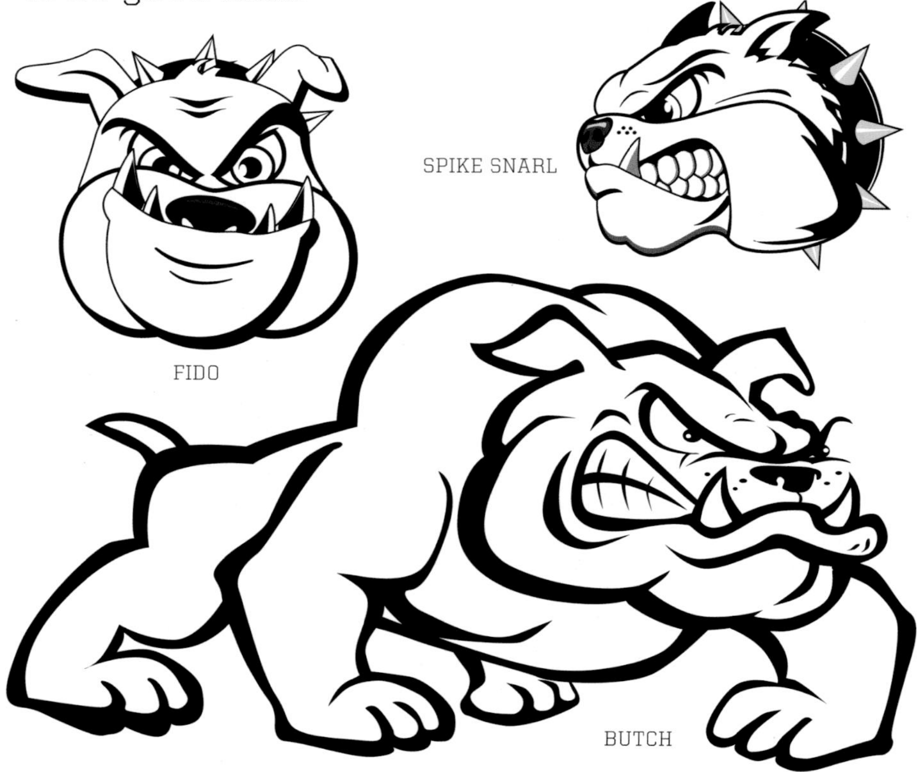

SPIKE SNARL

FIDO

BUTCH

BLACK SPIKE

GRRRRRR!

SPIKE

ROTWEILLER

FLORAL DOG

TRIBAL DOG

DOG HEAD

ROTWEILLER SWISH

ALSATIAN BARK

WESTIE

FAITHFUL FRIEND

CHINESE DOG

TERRIER

WILD DOG

DOLPHINS

Dolphin tattoos may symbolize several things; wisdom, freedom and even a love of the open waters. According to the Celtic belief, water has the power to cleanse the soul and rejuvenate. Therefore, people making a new start may choose to have a dolphin tattoo to symbolize a new life.

LEAPING DOLPHIN

DOLPHIN IN THE ROUND

FLIPPER

TRIBAL DOLPHIN

COMMON DOLPHIN

WHIRLING DOLPHINS

SIMPLE DOLPHIN

SINUOUS CETACEANS

DRAGONS

A dragon tattoo is a striking symbol of power, strength, courage and a protector of sacred items. Dragons are a good choice for a tattoo because they are sinuous and fluid. They do not have sharp edges or corners and, therefore, can be drawn to mould to any part of the body.

CHINESE DRAGON

GREEN DRAGON

CHINESE FANTAIL

SPEAR-TAIL

SEA DRAGON

RED DRAGON

YIN AND YANG

DRAGON ROUGE I

DRAGON ROUGE II

FORKED-TAIL

BLUE SEA DRAGON

DRAGON BANNER

DRAGON ROUGE III

DRAGON ROUGE IV

CIRCULAR DRAGON

SINUOUS CHINESE DRAGON

BLUE DRAGON

DRAGON RING

TRADITIONAL DRAGON

SERPENT DRAGON

DRAGON ROAR

ETHNIC DRAGON

FAIRIES

In literature, fairies often represent the personification of human desires in the form of little people with magical powers. As a tattoo design they can be symbols of youthful innocence and a desire to retain a child-like imagination, wonder and awe.

SEATED FAIRY

SMALL ORNATE FAIRY

ORNATE FAIRY

MAGICAL FAIRIES

RAINBOW FAIRY

TRIBAL FAIRY

GRACE AND BEAUTY

BLUEBELL FAIRY

FISH

Fish as tattoos have very many different meanings, depending on the fish you choose. For example, a Koi carp is a symbol of courage and masculinity. Siamese fighting fish are known to be aggressive and as a result have to be kept in their own tanks. This type of fish as a tattoo may be appropriate for a person who views themself as a loner. Other fish can represent a peaceful, sensitive person.

SIAMESE FIGHTING FISH

WHITE KOI
BLACK KOI

KOI WITH SPLASH

ANGEL FISH

TIGER FISH

MANTA RAY

ANGEL SILHOUETTE

GOLDFISH BUBBLES

GOLDFISH

KOI WAVES

BIG BAD FISH

SEAHORSE
CLOWNFISH
REEF FISH

LOBSTER

ANGLER FISH

WAVE FISH

FLAMES

Fire is a symbol of untamed energy. Whether as part of a sun motif or incorporated into a design of another object, flames with their undulating and sometimes tortuous curves bring a sense of movement and life to a design. They provide an ideal opportunity to use fiery colours – reds, oranges and yellows – in a tattoo.

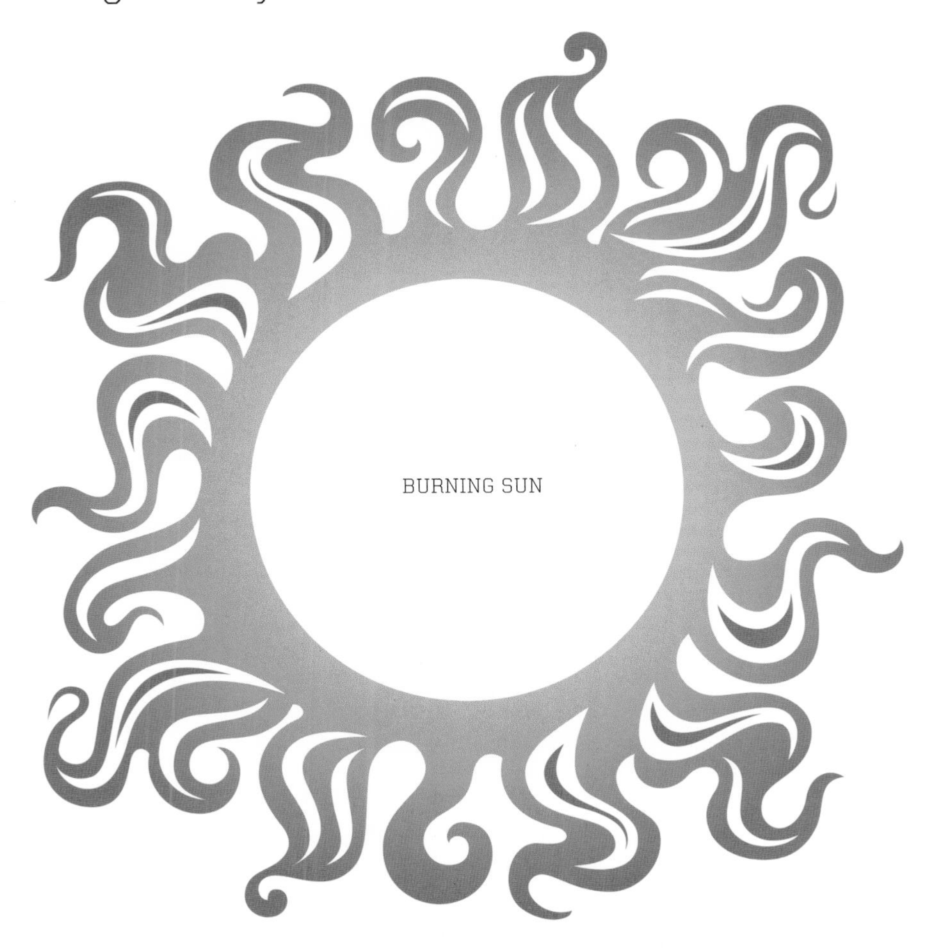

BURNING SUN

SMOKIN'

FIREBIRD

FLAMIN' GRIFFIN

TRIBAL FIRE

FIRE SWIRL

PHOENIX

ICE PHOENIX
FIRE DOG

RAGING INFERNO

HOTROD

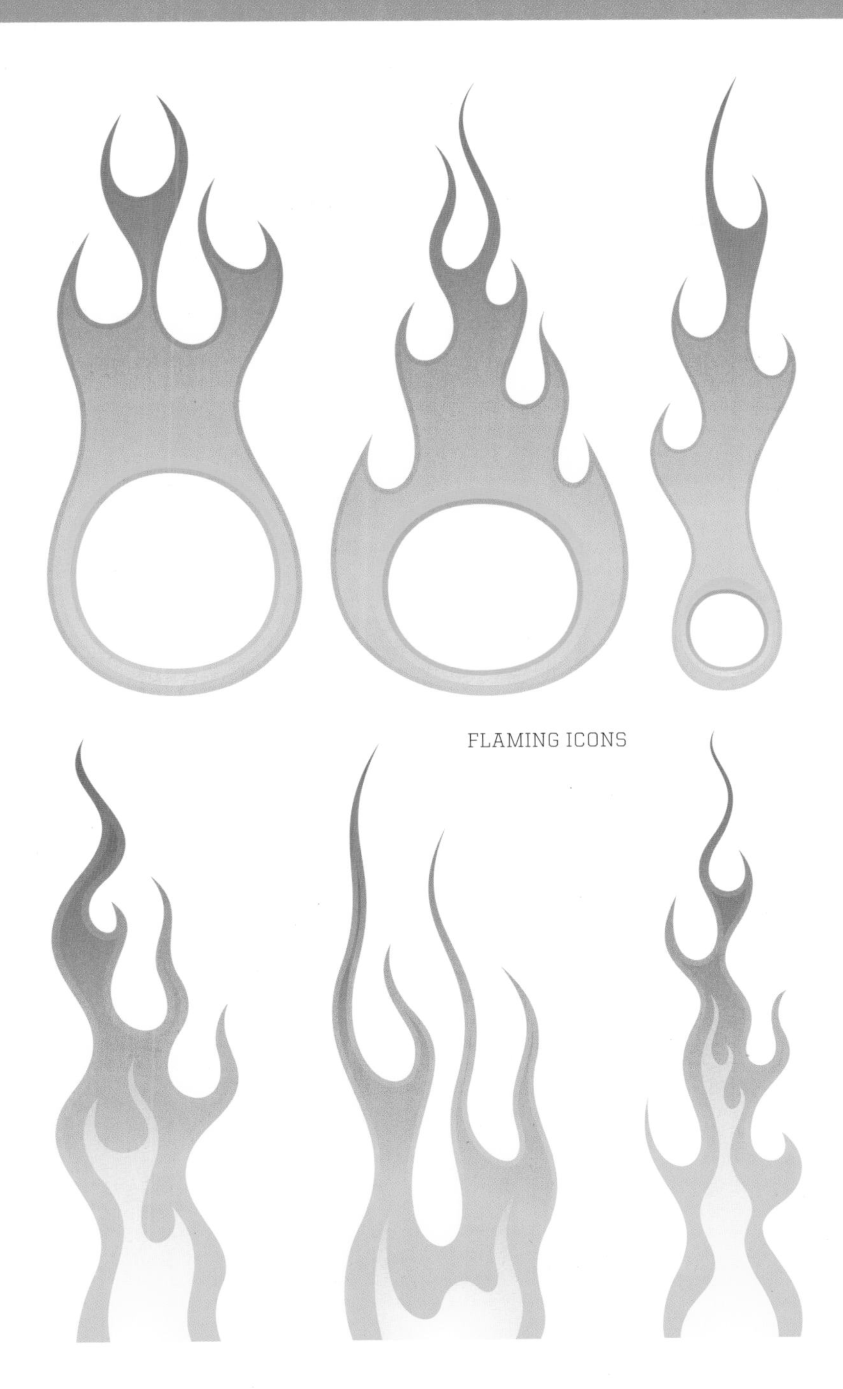

FLAMING ICONS

FLOURISHES

Swirls and curls, sometimes suggestive of plant tendrils or leaves, are a mainstay of tattoo art. They can be used to create designs of all shapes and dimensions to fit any body part, whether on their own or as an element of another design. Choose delicate or bold lines according to the effect you want to achieve.

TRADITIONAL FLOURISHES

FLORAL FLOURISHES

GARDEN FLOURISHES

LEAF FLOURISH

STALK AND BERRY

WAVE

FLOWERS

Flower tattoos are a good choice for a woman as a first tattoo. They can be pretty and delicately feminine, but you can have them made bigger and bolder, either as a single flower or as a chain.

Flowers are full of symbolism, so choose your design wisely. Red roses stand for love, romance and courage; pink roses represent grace; white roses signify eternal love and innocence. Lilies represent purity, and in ancient Egypt were a symbol of fertility. The calla lily signifies beauty, with orange petal lilies denoting passion. Daisy tattoos are very feminine, the flower representing innocence and loyalty in love. They are usually used small in tattoos.

MULTI-FLORA

FLOWERING CLIMBER

FLORAL EXPLOSION

DAISY

EVENING STAR

FLOWERHEAD

BERRY BUSH I

BERRY BUSH II

MORNING GLORY

TRIBAL BLUEBELL

LEAF FLOWER

WHITE ROSE
RED ROSE

ROSE I

ROSE II

ROSE III

LILY I

LILY II

LILY III

FROGS

Frogs are often seen as a symbol of regeneration, life and harmony. In ancient Egypt the frog was perceived to be a guide to the afterlife, while according to the traditions of some indigenous Americans, the frog brings rain. If you opt for a frog tattoo and want to be a bit edgy in your choice, then you can choose a tattoo of one of the beautiful but deadly poisonous frogs.

GREEN TREEFROG

TOAD

POISON DART FROGS

FROG SILHOUETTE

CLIMBING TREEFROG

PATTERNED FROG

ETHNIC FROG I

ETHNIC FROG II

GRIFFINS

With the head and wings of an eagle, and the body of a lion, the griffin (or gryphon) is a mythical beast, often seen in heraldry, associated with ideas of power and kingship. Sometimes shown with lion's claws or with eagle's talons, you can choose your own interpretation.

GOLDEN GRIFFIN

BLACK GRIFFIN

GRIFFIN RAMPANT

WHITE GRIFFIN

WINGED GRIFFIN

GUITARS

A modern-day icon, a guitar tattoo can be used to indicate the wearer's affinity with the rock music - usually heavy metal - scene. Decorated with wings, flames or the symbols of musical notation, the guitars themselves can be realistic renditions of actual instruments or stylized silhouettes.

MEGA-MIX

FLYING GUITAR

GRUNGE GUITAR

FLAMENCO GUITAR I

FLAMENCO GUITAR II

HEARTS

The ultimate symbol of love a heart is a classic vehicle for a tattooed statement of commitment to a special person in your life. Embellished with wings, swirling pennants, flowers and foliage, arrows and a myriad other design devices, hearts are an ever-popular choice.

WINGED HEART

FLAMING HEART

LOVE HEART

HEART SHAPES

LIGHT HEARTED

DAGGER THROUGH THE HEART

LIGHT HEARTED

BAROQUE HEART

FLYING HEART

DOUBLE LOVE

PURPLE HEART

BEDAZZLED

LOVE CONQUERS ALL

HERALDRY

Heraldic images are those motifs – often animals – that have through the ages been used on the coats of arms of the aristocracy to identify the wearer's family and military allegiances. In the Middle Ages when all-covering armour made combatants indistinguishable, the heraldic symbols emblazoned on their shields and standards were key to identification on the field of battle. The shield device has survived as part of the tattoo artist's repertoire, usually incorporating wings.

FLEUR DE LYS I

EAGLE

FLEUR DE LYS II

EAGLE AND AXE

FLYING SHIELD I

FLYING SHIELD II

EAGLE WITH ROUNDED WINGS

HERALDIC WINGS

EAGLE WITH OVAL WINGS

TWO-HEADED BIRD WITH CROWN

PHOENIX

EAGLE WITH SHIELD I

EAGLE WITH SHIELD II

HORSES

Horses have been depicted throughout history in many works of art and in many different forms. Horses signify strength, stamina, grace, beauty, nobility and freedom. A tattoo of a horse is a good way to symbolize a free spirit. The horse is such a beautiful animal and striking tattoo designs can be a very powerful way to express your fascination with this amazing creature.

STALLION OVAL

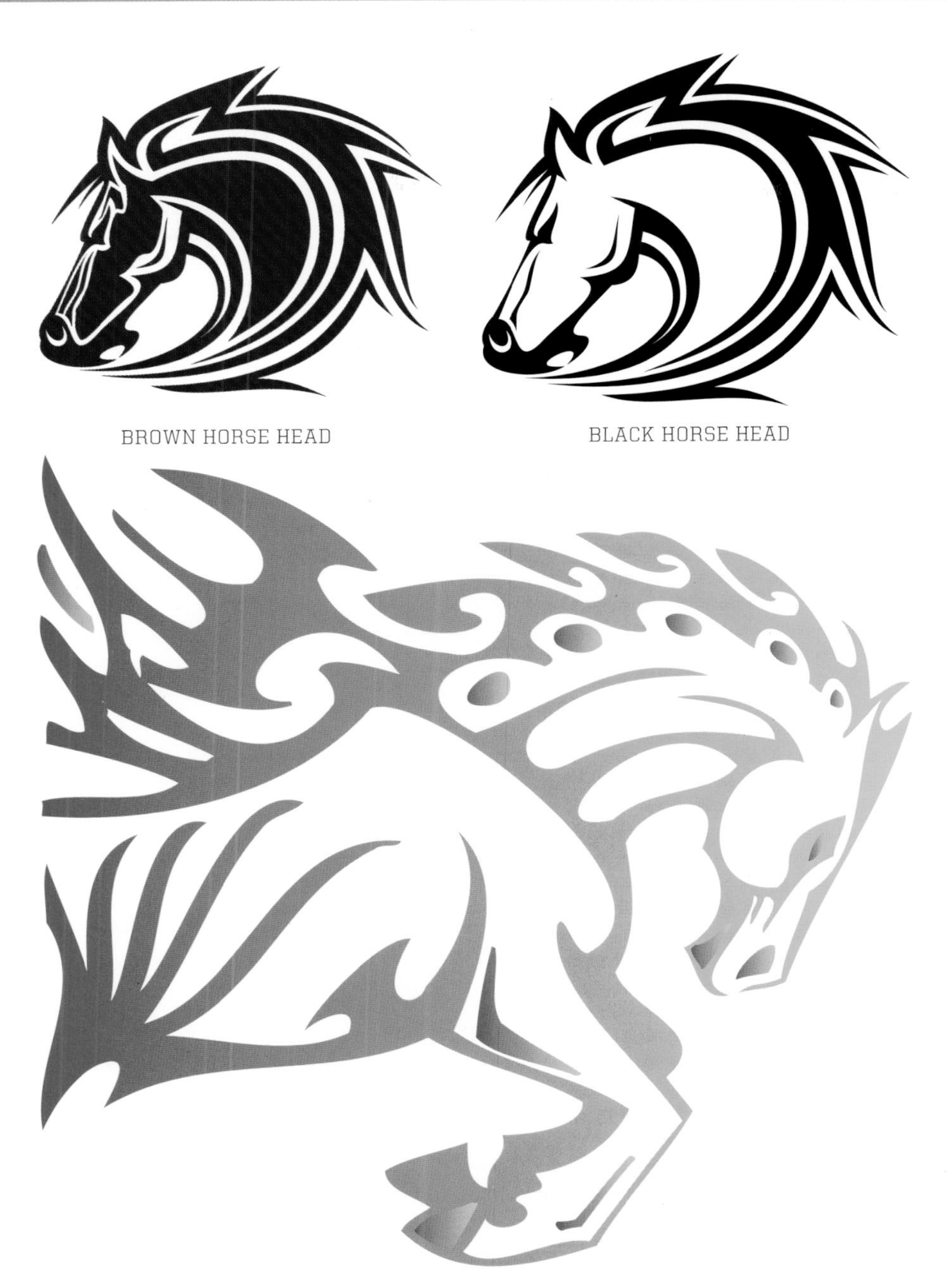

BROWN HORSE HEAD

BLACK HORSE HEAD

FLAMIN' HORSE

PRANCING

UNICORN

WILD MUSTANG
PONY
WINGED HORSE

CIRCULAR HORSE

TRIBAL HORSE GALLOPING

HORSE'S HEAD

REARING HORSE

INSECTS

There are over 800,000 species of insect, ranging from really disgusting to amazingly beautiful, so you certainly won't be short of inspiration if you decide to have an insect tattoo. You can have simple outlines, or more intricate shading with colour fill. The most popular of insect tattoos are the scarab beetle and the ladybird. The ladybird is said to bring you luck if it lands on you and certain cultures attribute them with healing powers. Scarab symbolism dates back to early Egyptian myths and are seen to signify rebirth or regeneration and protection.

LADYBIRDS

STYLIZED LADYBIRD

WINGED SCARAB
TRIBAL SCARAB
GREEN BEETLE

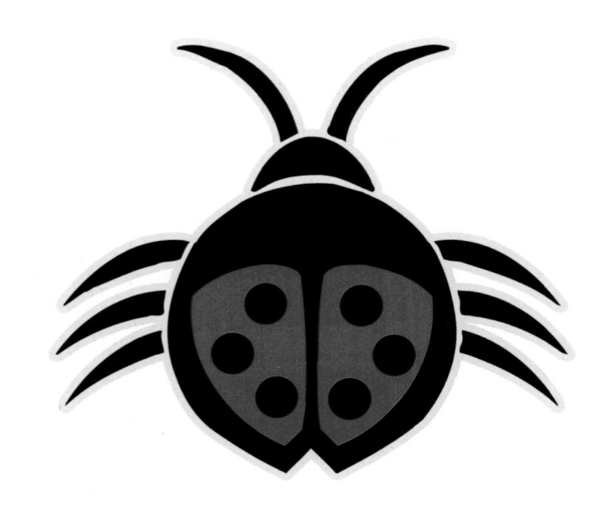

LADYBIRD

FLYING BUG I

MOTH I

BEE

FLYING BUG II

BUG

LADYBUG

MOTH II

BEETLE

STAG BEETLE

BROWN MOTH

LATTICE BUG

ANT

MOTH III

MOTH IV

RAINBOW DRAGONFLY

TRIBAL DRAGONFLY

ORIENTAL DRAGONFLY

OCEANIC DRAGONFLY

LIZARDS

In Shamanism the lizard is associated with 'dream time' and the link between the dream world and reality. They are said to indicate foresight and ancient knowledge. Their swirling forms echo a connection with ideas of illusiveness and agility. In tattoos they can be rendered in bold, sinuous outline forms, sometimes incorporating decorative geometric body markings.

LIZARD DANCE

TRIBAL LIZARD

GREEN LIZARD

LIZARD RING

BLUE LIZARD

MONITOR LIZARD

SAND LIZARD

ETHNIC LIZARD

LOUNGE LIZARD

LONG-TAILED LIZARD

GECKO

TRIBAL GECKO

MONKEYS

In Chinese astrology monkeys represent cleverness and curiosity. Left to their own devices, they can get into a lot of trouble. Their inventiveness can lead to good, or evil. They are quick and keen witted, observant, curious, loving and excellent in small business ventures. In tattoos decorative capital can be made from their long tails and limbs, as well as their fur and markings.

PIGGY-BACK

TROUBLE X3

TRIBAL GORILLA

BLACK MONKEY

WHITE MONKEY

HAPPY MONKEY

MONKEY PUZZLE

SHARKS

Fearless focus and independence of spirit are among the qualities we associate with sharks. They are seen as supreme survivors. Shark people are said to be adept at summing up and adapting to social situations as well as manipulating people and events. Tattoos of these creatures often incorporate decoration suggestive of their ocean environment: flowing and swirling currents and whirlpools.

BLUE FIN

TIGER SHARK

THRASHER

RIPPLED SHARK

HAMMERHEAD

TRIBAL SHARK

SKULLS

The ultimate horror symbol, skulls can never completely escape an association with death, danger and a disregard for convention and a safe life. They are often used on their own, perhaps surrounded by flames or with wings, as a 'full on' gothic statement. A skull can also be incorporated as an element in more complex device.

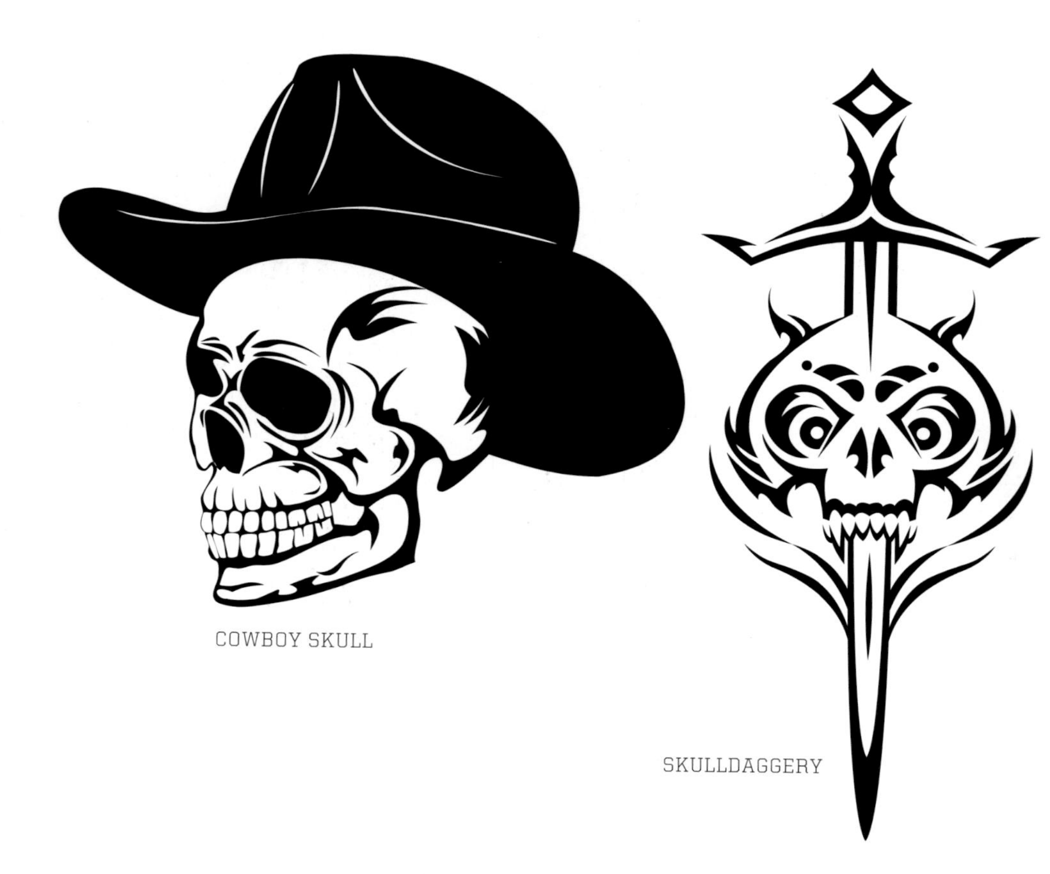

COWBOY SKULL

SKULLDAGGERY

RAZORTOOTH

FLAMIN' SKULL

MOTORSKULL

FLYING SKULL

BUTTERFLY SKULL

CELTIC WINGED SKULL

GREY-WINGED SKULL

TRIBAL SKULL

TRIBAL BIKER SKULL

SCREAMING SKULL

BARBED-WIRE AND BONES

BIRD SKULL

SKULL IN THE ROUND

CHOPPER SKULL

DEVIL SKULL

SKULLS AND DAGGER

GREEN-EYED SKULL

THE GRIM REAPER

GRUNGE SKULL

SNAKES

In Chinese culture, each animal is associated with certain personality traits and people born in the year of the snake are perceived to be calm and gentle, romantic and perceptive. Buddhist mythology depicts snakes as guardians. As snakes shed their skin regularly, snake tattoos also represent renewal and rebirth. Don't forget though that snakes are often portrayed as being dangerous, after all the Bible tells us that it was a serpent who tempted Adam and Eve and the forked tongue of the snake represents one who tells lies.

COBRA HEAD I

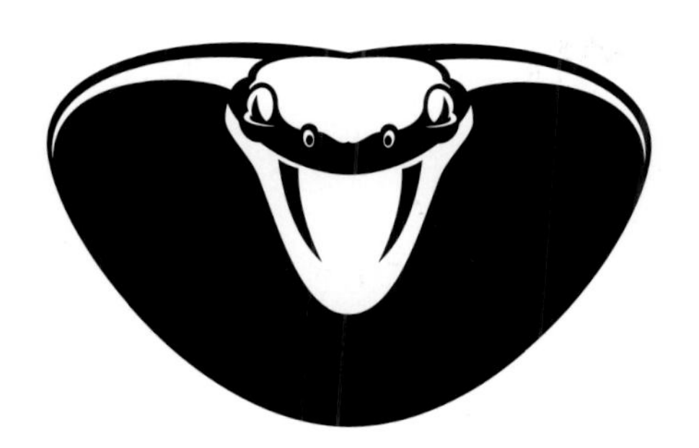

COBRA HEAD II

COBRA HEAD III

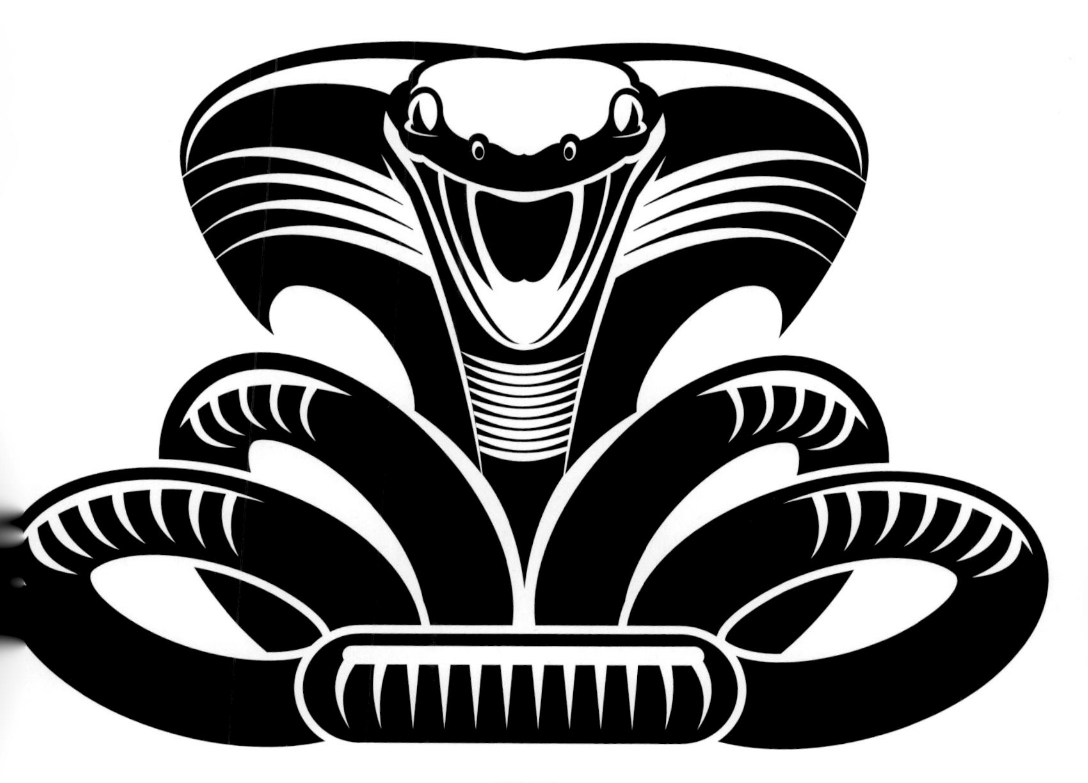

COBRA

CADUCEUS

COILED COBRA

COBRA STRIKE

SNAKE HEAD

COBRA

WHITE SNAKE

SNAKE, DAGGER, FLAMES AND SKULL

SERPENTIUM

SNAKE AND SWORD

SPIDERS

Associated with treachery and death in many cultures, spiders are seen as 'tricksters' in African traditions and a 'spinner of fate' in many ancient goddess cultures. In the West spiders have been viewed as an evil force that sucked blood from its victims, but sometimes as a symbol of good luck because of the cross on the back of some species. The Chinese have welcomed the spider descending on its thread as a bringer of joys from heaven. In design terms, the eight legs that surround the central body of the spider – and their webs – offer many decorative possibilities for tattoos.

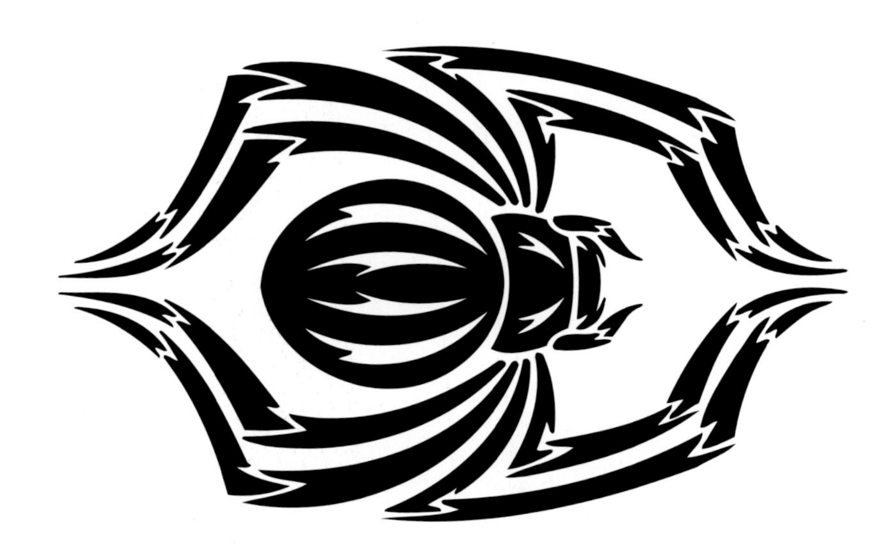

TRIBAL TARANTULA

CLOWN SPIDER

HOURGLASS ARACHNID

TRIBAL SPIDER

MASKED SPIDER

WIDOW WEB

BLACK WIDOW

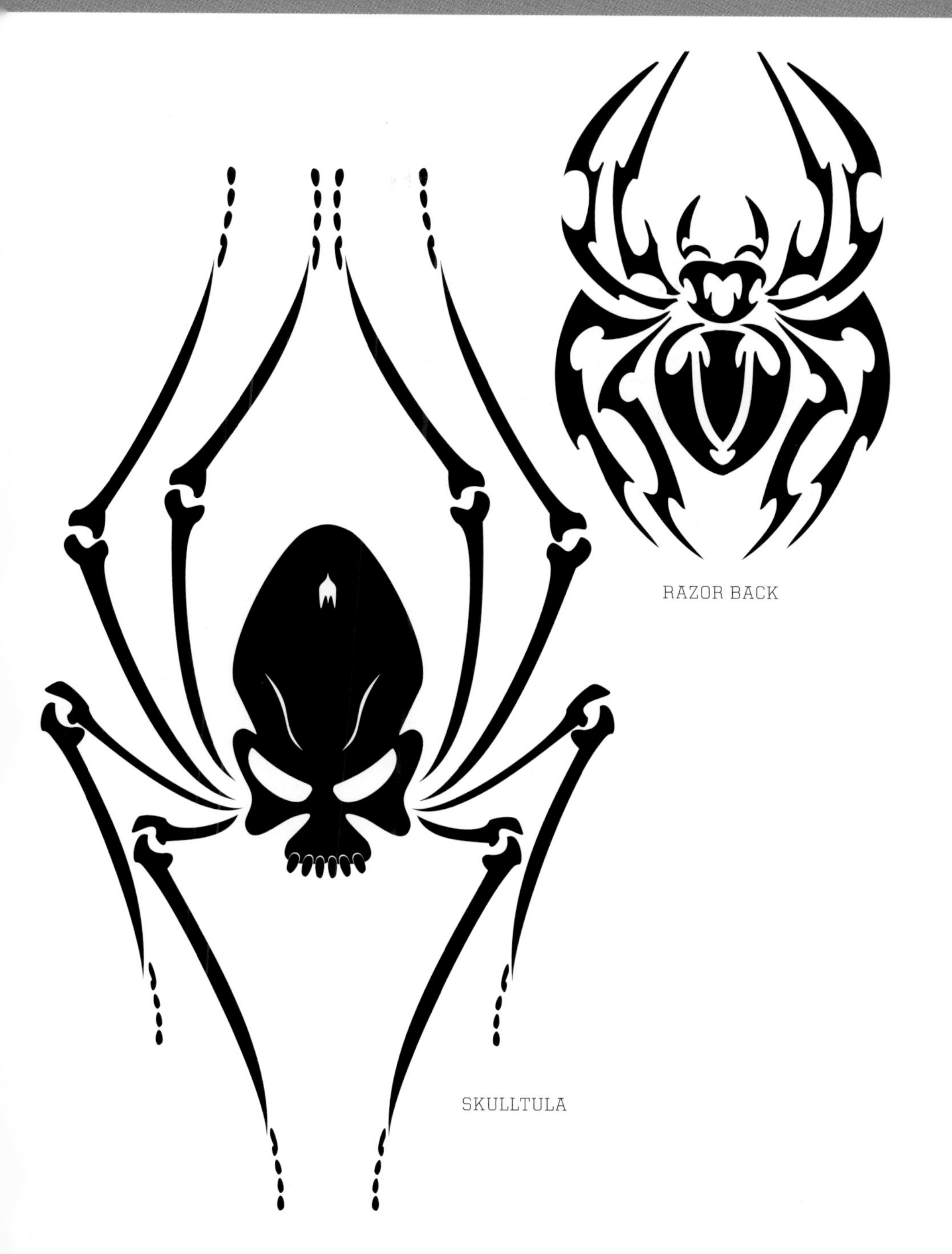

RAZOR BACK

SKULLTULA

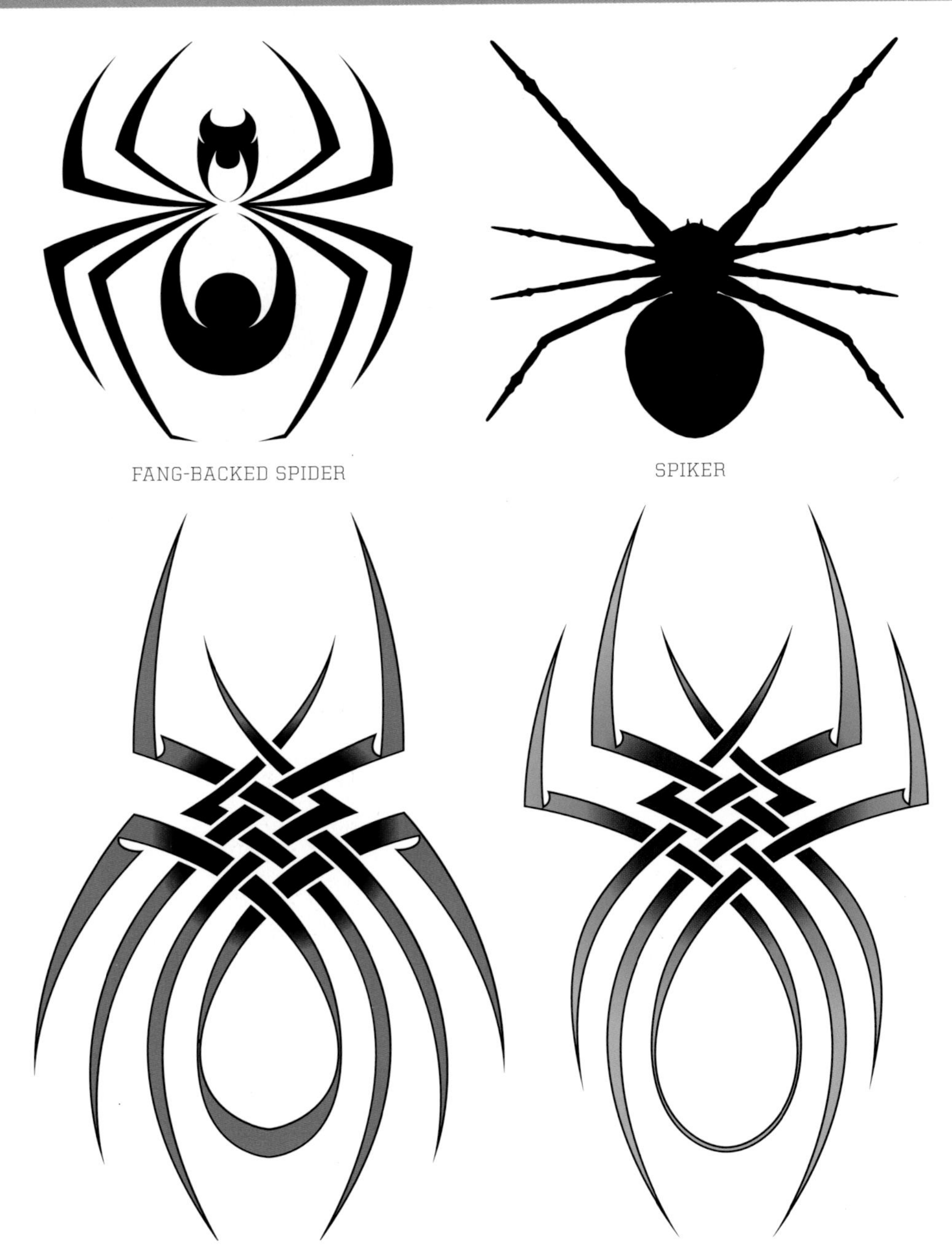

FANG-BACKED SPIDER

SPIKER

TRIBAL ARACHNIDS

ARACHNASKULL

HAPPY BACK
LANTERN SPIDER

SPIDER FANGS

SPIDER SYMMETRY

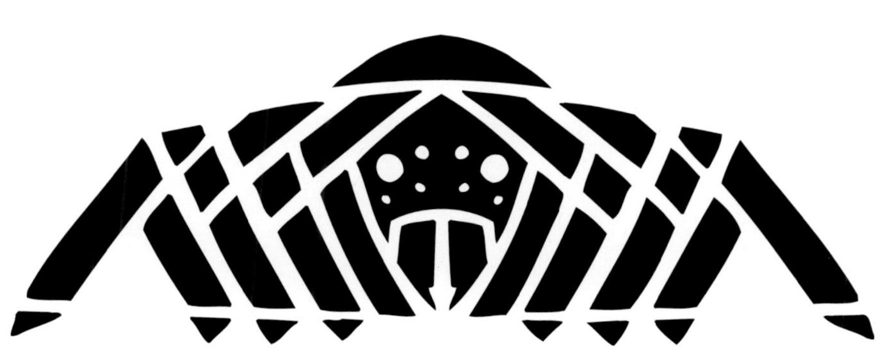

FACE-ON

SUNS

Power, energy, heat and light are all associated with the Sun. Our nearest star can also be seen as the source of life. Often depicted in tattoos with flames radiating from the centre, the Sun can also be shown in a variety of geometric forms.

HOT, HOT, HOT

STYLIZED SUN

FUN SUN I

FUN SUN II

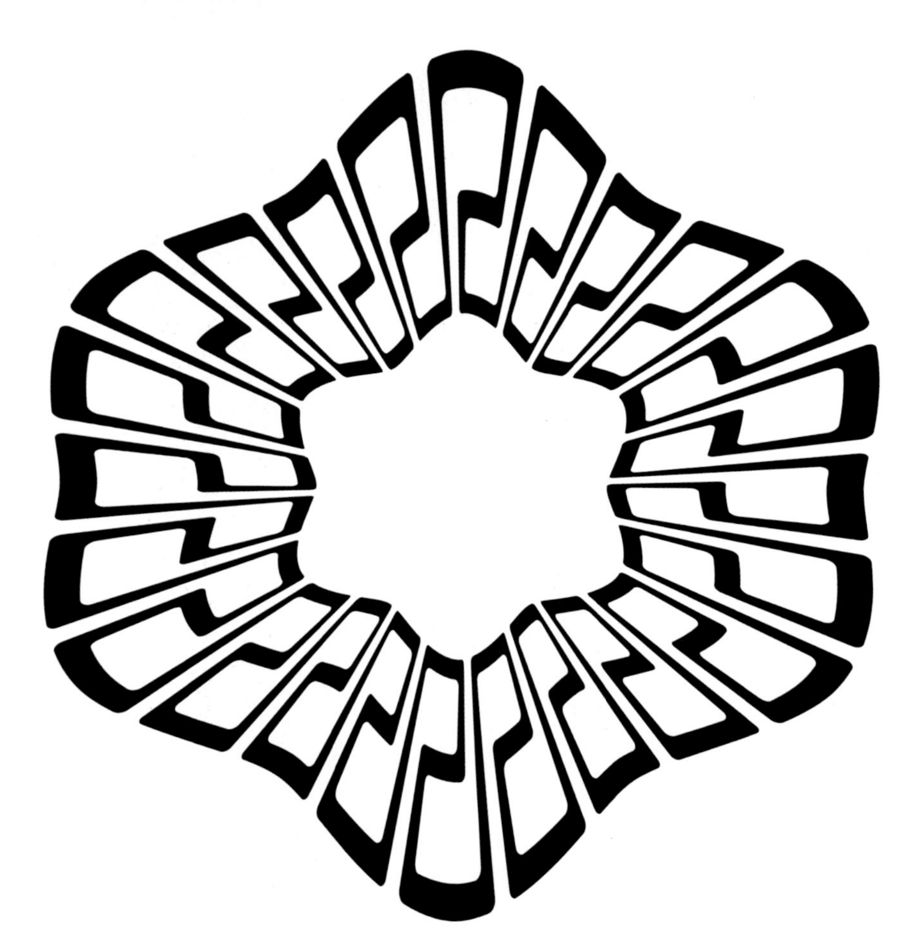

MODERN SUN

SUNS I

SUNS II

AZTEC SUN

ROTATING SUN
BURNING SUN

TRIBAL SUN I

TRIBAL SUN II

SUNSEEKER

TRIBAL SUNS

SUNS III

STARBURST

WINGS

Wing tattoos are very popular and appear in many different forms and mean different things to each wearer. They most commonly represent speed, freedom and aspiration. You can have wings of angels, birds, butterflies, fairies, dragonflies and many mythological winged creatures. The most common place to have a wing tattoo is on the back, taking up the width of the shoulders, although you can of course have much smaller ones on other parts of the body.

FEATHERED WINGS

ANIMAL WINGS

SPREAD WINGS
ANGEL WINGS

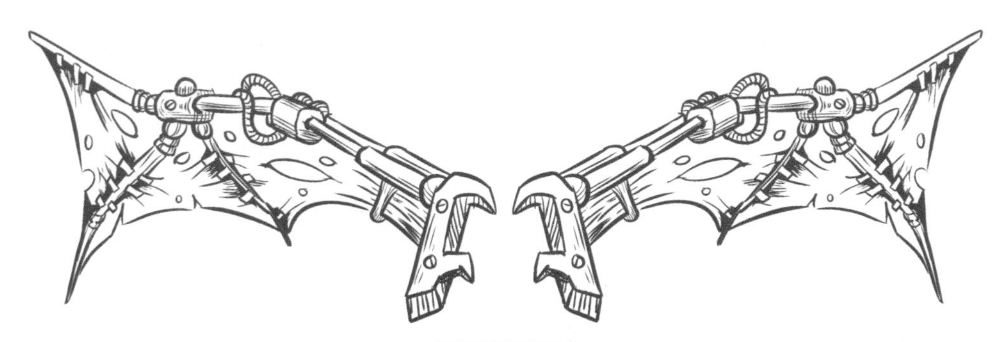

JUNK WINGS I

JUNK WINGS II

STONE WINGS

BONED WINGS

SWIRLED WINGS

PATTERNED WINGS

NATIVE WINGS

SOARING WINGS

BUTTERFLY WINGS

TRIBAL WINGS

DEMON BAT WINGS

BAT WINGS

DRAGON WINGS

HARPY WINGS

WOLVES

In Native American culture, wolves are seen as pathfinders and symbolize ancestors or other spiritual guides. Wolves are attributed with devotion, loyalty, fearlessness, intelligence; they are attuned to nature; and are pack (family) oriented. Wolf tattoos are inspirational and beautiful and are often seen to be the sign of strength and leadership.

TRIBAL WOLF HEAD

WOLF SWIRL

WOLF RING

THE HOWL

WOLF ATTACK

THE POUNCE

WOLF HEAD

BLACK WOLF

ALASKAN HOWL

HOWLING AT THE MOON

SNARL

CURIOUS WOLF

STALKING WOLF

LUPUS HEAD

TRIBAL WOLF

ZODIAC

The 12 Sun Signs of the Zodiac are among the most popular choices for tattoo designs. They provide an instantly understandable personal symbol for the wearer, relating to the position of the Earth in relation to the planets and stars at the time of their birth. The most familiar designs for the signs of the Zodiac have evolved over many centuries. But there is no reason why you can't use an innovative new design for your tattoo.

CAPRICORN

SCORPIO

GEMINI

ARIES

PISCES
LIBRA
CANCER
SAGITTARIUS
LEO
VIRGO
AQUARIUS
TAURUS

ARIES

TAURUS

CANCER

LEO

LIBRA

SCORPIO

CAPRICORN

AQUARIUS

PISCES

GEMINI

VIRGO

SAGITTARIUS

ARIES

TAURUS

GEMINI

LEO

VIRGO

LIBRA

SAGITTARIUS

CAPRICORN

AQUARIUS

CANCER

SCORPIO

PISCES

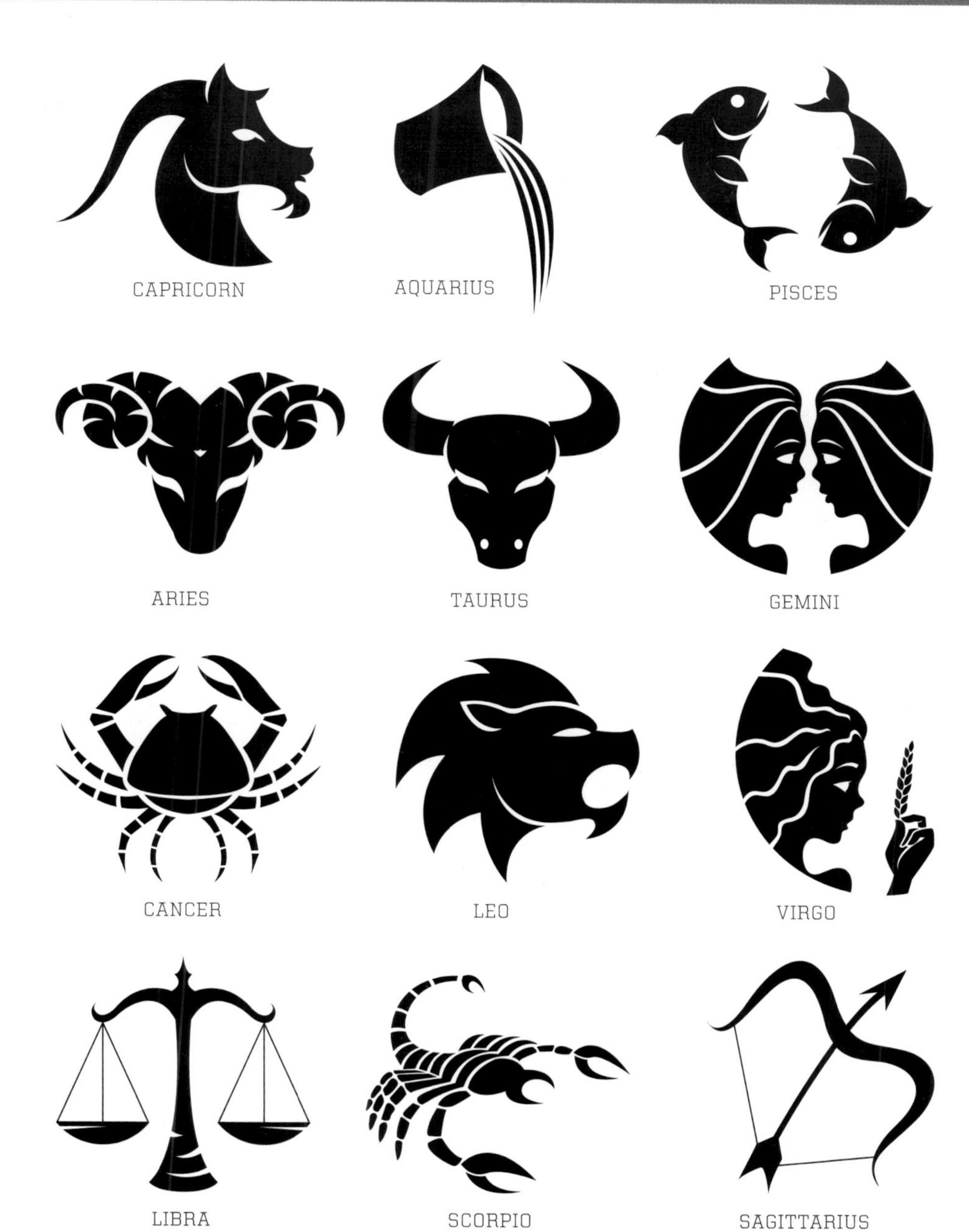
CAPRICORN
AQUARIUS
PISCES
ARIES
TAURUS
GEMINI
CANCER
LEO
VIRGO
LIBRA
SCORPIO
SAGITTARIUS

ARIES

TAURUS

LEO

LIBRA

AQUARIUS

CAPRICORN

GEMINI

CANCER

SAGITTARIUS

PISCES

SCORPIO

VIRGO

Acknowledgements

2 c Gigel **5** br Davor Ratkovic **6** bc margita **7** c Gizele **9** bc Allaua Heraldry **10** c karlovserg **11** Anchors **12** bl cr Seamartini Graphics **13** tr c, cr Seamartini Graphics **14** tl tr, cb Seamartini Graphics, youlikeit **15** tl, tr bl br thinkTHINGS, Seamartini Graphics **16** tl, tr b, bl br Olga Rutko, Seamartini Graphics, jazzia Angels **17** bl, c jagoda, niki2die4 **18** tl tr bl bc br AZ **19** tc, bc Vitezslav Halamka, Mila Petkova Automotive **20** tc, bc Siempreluca, Elisanth **21** tc, bc Mechanik **22** tc, bc Rikko, Yobidaba **23** tl tr bl br Sergey Prygov **24** tc bc Sergey Prygov **25** tc bc Sergey Prygov Aztecs **26** bc Lukiyanova Natalia / frenta **27** tl tr, bc Betacam-SP, Lukiyanova Natalia / frenta **28** c Artem Efimov **29** tc, bc aroas, Betacam-SP **30** tc, c, bl attem, Christos Georghiou, Lukiyanova Natalia/frenta **31** c aroas **32** tc bc Lukiyanova Natalia / frenta **33** tc bl, br Lukiyanova Natalia / frenta, Nekiy Banners **34** bc Bukhavets Mikhall **35** c Bukhavets Mikhall **36** tc, bc Allaua, Sergio Hayashi **37** c Olga Rutko Bats **38** tc, bc John Lock **39** c Johny Keny **40** bc Labetskiy Alexandr Alexandrovich, Sergey Prygov **41** tc, c, b S. Hanusch, Sergey Prygov, Irina Mikhaylova **42** tc, bc Evgeniya Rodina **43** tc bc Evgeniya Rodina, Makhnach Birds **44** kokitom, Tyurin Ruslan **45** t b Matamu **46** t b Matamu **48** c John Lock **49** t b frescomovie **50** tc, bc Sferdon **51** tc bc frescomovie **52** tc bc Tee Scott, cartoons **53** bl tr Seamartini Graphics **54** tc bc Seamartini Graphics, Peregudov Dmytro **55** tc, bc Seamartini Graphics, Jennifer Johnson, BlueCherry Graphics **56** tc bc karlovserg, Terry Chan **57** tr, c, bl Advent, Sergey Prygov, Labetskiy Alexandr Alexandrovich **58** tl, br bl Matamu, Sergey Prygov, erdem **59** tc, bc Vallentin Vassileff, cartoons **60** tl, cr, b victor roberto ojeda, Aljulew, L.L.C.vieira72 **61** c Sergey Prygov **62** c, b Sergey Prygov, AKV **63** c Viktoria **64** t, b Seamartini Graphics, **65** tl,tr,bl,br silvano audisio **66** t,b Kopirin **67** c silvano audisio, DeepGreen **68** c Gizele **69** t, bl,br paul_june, frescomovie **70** t, b Artpoint **71** tl,tr,b Seamartini Graphics Cats **72** bc Dimiter Petrov **73** bl, cr Danylchenko Iaroslav **74** tc, bc Bastetamon, frescomovie **75** tl, tr, bc Galitsyn, DmitryPrudnichenko, pixelcraft **76** tl tr, bc Galitsyn, Sferdon, Karina Cornelius **77** c Spyder **78** c Sapik **79** tc, c, bl, br YnM Creations, krabata, Sergey Prygov, Seamartini Graphics **80** c victor roberto ojeda **81** tc bl br Galitsyn Celtic **82** bc Natalia Cebotari **83** tl tr cl cr bl br Alvaro Cabrera Jimenez **84** t, b Nekiy **85** tc, bc Nekiy, Rehman **86** tl tr, cl c cr bl br Olan, Alvaro Cabrera Jimenez **87** tl tr cl c cr bl br Alvaro Cabrera Jimenez **88** c Tee Scott **89** tc, bc Nekiy, ChaosMaker Chinese **90** bc szefei **91** tl, tr, bl, br fotohunter **92** c Losswen Circles **93** bc John David Bigl III **94** tc bc John David Bigl III **95** tc, bl br Ellin, Amenhotepov **96** tl br joingate **97** tl tr bc joingate Crocodiles **96** c bc Sergey Prygov **97** c patrimonio designs limited Dogs **98** tl tr bc mirabile **99** tl, tr bc mirabile, Brad Collett **100** tl, tr, bc Seamartini Graphics, Unavailable, Gipnos **101** tc, bc Unavailable, Seamartini Graphics **102** tl, tr, bc Allied Computer Graphics, Inc., Ovchynnikov Oleksii, Kopirin **103** tl bc, tr John Lock, Unavailable Dolphins **104** tr, bl advent, Osipovev **105** tc, c, bc Unavailable, Phoenix1983 **106** tc, bc Steyno&Stitch, Sferdon **107** tl tr bl br bomg Dragons **108** bc Gigel- **109** tc, bc margita, frescomovie **110** c shadow216 **111** tl, br frescomovie, Davor Ratkovic **112** tc, bl br Boguslaw Mazur, MisterElements **113** tc c, bc frescomovie, Bastetamon **114** tl tr, bc MisterElements, frescomovie **115** c John Lock **116** tl tr, bc relishtheglamour, Sahua d **117** tl, cr, bc igor kisselev, relishtheglamour, Zuzuan Fairies **118** c Triling Studio Ltd **119** tl, tr, bl Olena Tkachenko **120** tl tr br, cl OzZon **121** tr, bl Nanna Design, Bastetamon **122** bc Triling Studio Ltd Fish **123** bc cartoons **124** l, r Christos Georghiou **125** tl, br margita, ksysha **126** tc, cr, bl br Unavailable, Abrakadabra **127** tr, bl Kess **128** c ksysha **129** tl, tr cr bl br Bomg, Alegria **130** tc c, bc ksysha, Tasika, Kazyavka Flames **131** l, tr cr bcr br rojo **132** t, ct, bc b artpoint, Bastetamon **133** tc, c, bc Bastetamon **134** l, r artpoint, Bastetamon **135** bl, tr Bastetamon **136** tc, bc MRG, Siempreluca **137** tl tc tr bl bc br cajoer Flourishes **138** c br jenkoh **139** l, tr cr bcr br Mad Dog, bazal78 **140** tl trctl ctr, c cb b glossygirl21, Maryna Radzionava **141** tc, c, b Olena Tkachenco, glossygirl21, RedGreen Flowers **142** bl, br MariStep, sergwsq **143** c Maryna Radzionava **144** tl cl, tr, bl br Albina Tiplyashina, Sergey Prygov, paul_june, **145** l tr, br Sergey Prygov, Albina Tiplyashina **146** t b Alexkava **147** t c b Sergey Prygov **148** tl tr b Sergey Prygov Frogs **149** bc Olga Rutko **150** t, b Vallentin Vassileff, Artur Tiutenko **151** bl tr karlovserg, Zara's gallery **152** t, bl br Lindwa, Betacam-SP Griffins **153** bc Spyder **154** tc, bc Matamu, Olga Rutko **155** tc, bc Nebojsa Dikic, mgstudio Guitars **156** b High Leg Studio **157** tc, bc Mariya Lebedinskaya **158** c Karlionau **159** l r jazzia Hearts **160** bc kokitom **161** tc, bc Anmax, tracie andrews **162** t c b ELENA_M **163** t, c b ELENA_M, Marco Hayashi **164** tc, bc karlovserg, Anmax **165** tc, bc Ela Kwasniewski, Gordan **166** tc, c bc RetroClipArt, Allaua **167** t cl cr, cb Smirnova Alexandra, Allaua Heraldry **168** c, bl br Marco Hayashi, paul_june **169** tc, bl br Marco Hayashi, Seamartini Graphics **170** tc bc Marco Hayashi, krabata **171** tc, bc Marco Hayashi, fractalgr **172** c Roberto Castillo **173** tc bc Ezepov Dmitry Horses **174** cl tr bc bl br Seamartini Graphics **175** tl tr, bc Seamartini Graphics, Sergey Prygov **176** tc bc Sergey Prygov **177** tc, bl, br Olga Itina, Seamartini Graphics, Phoenix 1983 **178** tr, bc advent, victor roberto ojeda **179** tc, br Oksanika, victor roberto ojeda Insects **180** tc, cl, bc Alhovik, Lack-O'Keen **181** tc, bl, br Olga Rutko, Kaetana, Ihnatovich Maryia **182** tc, c br Keene illustrations, Boordon **183** tc c bl br Boordon **184** tl tr bl br Boordon **185** tl tr bl br Boordon **186** tc, bc Ajay Shrivastava, MontgomeryQ **187** tc bc ksysha Lizards **188** c, bc silvano audisio **189** c Dimiter Petrov **190** tc bc Sergey Prygov **191** tl br Sergey Prygov **192** tl, tr, br nem4a, Betacam-SP, Osipovev **193** tl, r karlovserg, mart Monkeys **194** bc John Lock **195** t, bc Sergey Prygov, Damaratskaya Alena **196** tl, tr cr, cb Kopirin, Sergey Furtaev, frescomovie Sharks **197** c bc S. Hanusch **198** tc bc Seamartini Graphics **199** tc, bc Osipovev, kang Skulls **200** cl, cr SS1001, Alexkava **201** c SFerdon, **202** c D. Kusters **203** c Sergey Prygov **204** tl, br nix, Luther **205** tc, bc SS1001, High Leg Studio **206** tc, bc AKV, chen **207** l, tr, br relishtheglamour, SFerdon, Jef Thompson **208** tl, r, bl Galitsyn, Sergey Prygov, Unavailable **209** c Galitsyn **210** tl, br Bomg, Seamartini Graphics **211** c Hugolacasse Snakes **212** bc Seamartini Graphics **213** tl tr bc Seamartini Graphics **214** tl, tr, cb flankerd, toocrazy, goGOgo **215** tr bl, cr Allied Computer Graphics, Inc., OzZon, flankerd **216** c Gary Kroman **217** l, r Kopirin, karlovserg Spiders **218** bc Sergey Prygov **219** tl tr bl br Sergey Prygov **220** tc, br Sergey Prygov, humpkin **221** tr, bl Sergey Prygov, Gheorghe Bunescu Bogdan Mircea **222** tl, tr, bl,br Gizmer, NesaCera, bomg **223** c Lyubov Fayerfas **224** tc, bc Sergey Prygov, artpoint **225** tc c bc Sergey Prygov Suns **226** c bc mirabile **227** tc bl br nattalex **228** tc, bl bc br igor kisselev, nenadv **229** tl tc tr, bc nenadv, igor kisselev **230** tc, bc Siart, Ajay Shrivastava **231** tr bl Ajay Shrivastava **232** tc, c, bc Siart, Ajay Shrivastava **233** tc, cl, cr, bl, br nenadv, Sergey Prygov Wings **234** c bc High Leg Studio **235** tc bc Tshirt-Factory **236** tl tr, cl, br Tshirt-Factory **237** tl, bl, r Tshirt-Factory **238** tc, bc kenee **239** tc c bc jstan **240** tc, bc ksysha, shadow216 **241** tc c bc antipathique Wolves **242** bl, br Cartoons, Sergey Prygov **243** bl, tr Unavailable, advent **244** tl tr, cl, br Sergey Prygov, Rezvoi, Advent **245** tl, r, bl cvijovic zarko, Phoenix1983, Tee Scott **246** tc, bc Oorka, Pixelcraft **247** tc, bc SS1001, Sergey Prygov Zodiac **248** tl-br Bastetamon **249** tl-br Bastetamon **250** tl-br Bastetamon **251** tl-br Bastetamon **252** tl-br Bastetamon **253** tl-br Cihan Demirok, Cidepix **254** tl-br Baloncici **255** tl-br Baloncici Shutterstock

Cover image: Gary Kroman/iStockphoto

While every effort has been made to credit contributors, the publishers would like to apologize should there have been any omissions or errors – and would be pleased to make the appropriate correction for future editions of the book.